KENNETH GRAHAME'S

THE WIND IN THE WILLOWS

A SCRIPT FOR RADIO AND STAGE

READING

KENNETH GRAHAME'S

THE WIND IN THE WILLOWS

ADAPTED FOR RADIO AND STAGE READING

BY

BART MEEHAN

ArtSound Press

Canberra

ArtSound Press
Canberra, Australia
Website: ArtSound.fm
Contact: ArtSoundtheatre@gmail.com

OFirst published in Canberra, Australia by ArtSound Press 2023

Copyright © ArtSound FM

The moral right of the author has been asserted

Printed and bound by Ingram Sparks

ISBN: 978-0-645-76920-3

The Wind in the Willows by Kenneth Grahame was originally published in 1908 and has since become a beloved classic for the young and young at heart. This script adapts the novel for performance on both radio and stage.

The adaptation was originally produced by ArtSound FM, Australia, and broadcast in 2022. The original cast were:

Nikki Hunter as The Narrator

Elaine Noon as Mole

Geoffrey Borny as Rat

Graham Robertson as Badger

Tony Turner as Toad

Nigel Palfreman as Otter

Lainie Hart as The Gaoler's Daughter

Neil McLeod as The Magistrate and The Engine Driver

The cast also played other smaller roles.

The production was directed by Tony Turner with an original musical score by Glenn Gore Phillips.

A podcast of the serial is available at https://www.podomatic.com/podcasts/podcast11793

Enquiries about performance rights should be directed to ArtSoundtheatre@gmail.com

LIST OF CHARACTERS:

Narrator

Toad

Mole

Rat

Badger

Otter

The Magistrate

Gaoler's Daughter

Gaoler

Engine Driver

Driver 1 and Driver 2

Sergeant Stoat

Stoat

Notes

1. The Narrator's dialogue is shown in italics in the script.
2. The play was written for radio/podcast. However, it is suitable for dramatic readings, using minimal sets. For that reason the script does not include stage directions or set recommendations.

3. Sound effects (SFX) are listed to assist in radio or podcast productions
4. References to "Transition" within the script refer to a point where sound or music can be used to transition between scenes in the narrative.

ACT ONE

Mole had been working very hard all the morning, spring-cleaning his little home. First with brooms, then with dusters; then on ladders and steps and chairs, with a brush and a pail of whitewash; till he had dust in his throat and eyes, and splashes of whitewash all over his black fur. It was small wonder, then, that he suddenly flung down his brush on the floor.

Mole: Bother! Hang spring-cleaning!

… and he bolted out of the house without even waiting to put on his coat.

Mole: Up we go! Up we go!

He climbed and climbed until at last…Pop! his snout came out into the sunlight and he found himself rolling in the warm grass of a great meadow.

Mole: Well, this is fine! This is better than whitewashing! This really is too good to be true. Birds singing, flowers budding, leaves waving —everything happy, and progressive, and occupied.

He walked along thinking his happiness was complete when he suddenly found himself standing by the edge of a river.

The Mole was bewitched, entranced…fascinated!

He sat on the grass looking across the river and noticed a dark hole in the bank opposite, just above the water's edge.

Mole: That's a curious thing. Is that an eye winking at me? And is that face?

Rat: Hullo, Mole!

Mole: Hullo, Rat!

Rat: Would you like to come over.

Mole: And how do you suggest I do that?

The Rat said nothing, but stooped and unfastened a rope and hauled on it; then lightly stepped into a little boat which the Mole had not seen before and sculled smartly across the river.

Mole: Oh my. How wonderful. Do you know, I've never been in a boat before in all my life.

Rat: What? Never been in —you never—well I—what have you been doing, then?

Mole: You make it sound as though boating is the only thing to do.

Rat: Believe me, my young friend, there is *nothing*—absolutely nothing—half so much worth doing as simply messing about in boats. Simply messing—about—in—boats; messing—

Mole: Look ahead, Rat! Watch out.

But it was too late. The boat struck the bank full tilt.

Mole: Are you alright?

Rat: Fine, absolutely fine, my dear Mole. Boats! Marvellous things. Wonderful, truly wonderful. In or out of 'em, it doesn't matter. Nothing seems really to matter, that's the charm of it. Whether you get away, or whether you don't; whether you arrive at your destination or whether you reach somewhere else, or whether you never get anywhere at all, you're always busy, and you never do anything in particular; and when you've done it there's always something else to do, and you can do it if you like, but you'd much better not. Look here! If you've really nothing else on hand this morning, supposing we pack some lunch and go down the river together? We can make a day of it.

Mole: Really? Oh what a day I'm having! So much better than white washing. Can we start at once?

And so they did, with Mole intoxicated with the sparkle, the ripple, the scents and the sounds and the sunlight, as he trailed a paw in the water and dreamed long waking dreams, while Ratty like the good little fellow he was, sculled steadily on in silence so as not to disturb him.

Finally, it was Mole who broke the revery

Mole: I beg your pardon, Ratty. You'll think me very stupid; but all this is so new to me. So—this—is—a—River!

Rat: *The* River!

Mole: And you really live by it? What a jolly life!

Rat: By it and with it and on it and in it. It's brother and sister to me, and aunts, and company, and food and drink. It's my world, and I don't want any other. What it hasn't got is not worth having, and what it doesn't know is not worth knowing. Lord! the times we've had together!

Mole: But isn't it a bit dull at times? Just you and the river, and no one else to pass a word with?

Rat: No one else to...! —well, I mustn't be hard on you You're new to it, and of course you don't know. The bank is so crowded nowadays that many people are moving away altogether. Otters, king-fishers, dabchicks, moorhens, all of them about all day long and always wanting you to *do* something—as if a fellow had no business of his own to attend to!

Mole: What lies over *there*? It's very dark...

Rat: That? Oh, that's just the Wild Wood. We don't go there very much, we river-bankers.

Mole: Aren't they—aren't they very *nice* people in there?

Rat: W-e-ll, let me see. The squirrels are all right. *And* the rabbits—some of 'em, but rabbits are a mixed lot. And then there's Badger, of course. He lives right in the heart of it; wouldn't live anywhere else either, if you paid him to do it. Dear old Badger! Nobody interferes with *him*.

Mole: Why, who *should* interfere with him?

Rat: Weasels—and stoats—and foxes—and so on. They're all right in a way but they break out sometimes and you can't really trust them, and that's the fact.

Mole: And beyond the Wild Wood, where it's all blue and dim and you can see those ribbons of smoke?

Rat: Beyond the Wild Wood comes the Wide World, my young friend. And that's something that doesn't matter, either to you or me. I've never been there, and I'm never going, nor you either, if you've got any sense at all. People! Bah! Don't ever refer to it again, please. Now then, here's our backwater at last. We'll stop to have lunch.

Leaving the main stream, Mole and Ratty passed into what seemed at first sight like a little landlocked lake. Ratty brought the boat alongside the bank, helped the still awkward Mole safely ashore, and swung out a picnic basket.

Mole: Can I unpack our lunch, Ratty. I mean I have never done this before and I really want to experience everything… Oh it's marvellous, Ratty. And there's so much…

Rat: Really? It's only what I always take on these little excursions (*rushing through it*) coldchickencoldtonguecoldhamcoldbeefpickledgherkinssaladfrenc hrollscresssandwichespottedmeatgingerbeerlemonadesodawate…

Mole: (*laughing*) Oh stop! stop! I can't stand it…

Rat: (*good humoured*) Alright then, young Moley, I'll just stretch out here on the grass and leave you to it. You can call me when everything's ready.

Mole: Oh my, oh my…it's all so wonderful.

When all was ready, he woke Ratty and they ate and ate and ate until they were ready to burst and then patted their stomachs in satisfaction.

Rat: Well that was very fine. Very fine indeed. What are you looking at?

Mole: There's a streak of bubbles travelling along the surface of the water.

Rat: Bubbles?

A broad glistening muzzle showed itself above the edge of the bank, and the Otter hauled himself out and shook the water from his coat.

Otter: Greedy beggars! Why didn't you invite me, Ratty?

Rat: It was an impromptu affair, Otter. We just up and decided to go boating on the spur of the moment. By the way, this is my friend Mr. Mole.

Mole: I'm very pleased to meet you, Mr Otter.

Otter: Pleased to meet you as well. Such a rumpus everywhere! All the world seems out on the river to-day. I came up this backwater to try and get a moment's peace, and then stumble upon you fellows!

Mole: What's that moving there in the hedge, Ratty?

Rat: Why, it's old Badger.

The Badger trotted forward a pace or two, then grunted and turned his back and disappeared from view.

Mole: Oh my…

Rat: Don't be offended. That's *just* the sort of fellow he is. We shan't see any more of him to-day.

Mole: (*disappointed*) Oh dear, I would have liked to meet him!

Rat: You will, Mole. I'll invite him to dinner.

Otter: (*suddenly interested*) Dinner!

Rat: (*quickly changing the subject*). Never mind that. Tell us, Otter, *who's* out on the river?

Otter: Toad, for one. In his brand-new wager-boat; new togs, new everything!

Rat: (*laughing*) Once, it was nothing but sailing. Then he tired of that and took to punting. Nothing would please him but to punt all day and every day, and a nice mess he made of it. Last year it was house-boating, and we all had to go and stay with him in his house-boat, and pretend we liked it. He was going to spend the rest of his life in a house-boat. It's all the same, whatever he takes up; he gets tired of it, and starts on something new.

Otter: Such a good fellow, too, but no stability—especially in a boat!

Suddenly across the main stream they saw a boat flash into view, the rower—a short, stout figure—splashing badly and rolling a good deal.

Otter: Well speak of the devil (laughs)

Rat: He'll be out of that boat in a minute.

Otter: Of course he will (*chuckles*) Did I ever tell you that good story about Toad and the lock-keeper? It happened this way. Toad.... (*fades away as he seems to be distracted*)

An errant May-fly flew lazily over the river and in a sudden swirl of water the May-fly was visible no more. And neither was the Otter.

Mole: He's gone!

Rat: Nice fellow, but preoccupied with breakfast, lunch, dinner… oh, and supper. Well, well, I suppose we ought to be moving. I wonder which of us had better pack the luncheon-basket?

Mole: Oh, please let me.

And Ratty let him… but of course, packing the basket was not quite as pleasant as unpacking the basket. It never is.

The afternoon sun was getting low as Ratty sculled gently homewards in a dreamy mood, murmuring poetry-things to himself and not paying much attention to Mole.

Mole: Ratty?

Rat: Hmmm?

Mole: I do love the river, Ratty.

Rat: What's that, Moley? Oh yes, the river is splendid. Here's a thought. Why don't you come and stop with me for a little bit. It's very plain and rough, you know—not like Toad's house at all—but I can make you comfortable. And I'll teach you to row and to swim, and you'll soon be as handy on the water as any of us.

Mole: What a wonderful day. The very best of days…I will never waste another on spring cleaning …

It was true that this was the best of days but it was only the first of many for the emancipated Mole, each of them longer and full of interest as the ripening summer moved forward. He did learn to swim and to row, and entered into the joy of running water; and then lay on the bank, drying under the warm sun, while he listened to the whispering of the wind in the willows.

Mole: Ratty, this has all been so wonderful and you have been so kind, but I have a favour to ask.

Rat: *(off hand)* Ask away.

Mole: Will you take me to meet Mr. Toad? I've heard so much about him, and I do so want to make his acquaintance.

Rat: Toad? Ofcourse, what a splendid idea. Get the boat out, and we'll paddle up there at once. It's never the wrong time to call on Toad. Early or late, he's always the same fellow. Always good-tempered, always glad to see you, always sorry when you go!

Mole: He must be a very nice animal.

Rat: In his own way, I suppose he is. . Simple, good-natured, though perhaps not very clever—we can't all be geniuses; and it may be that he is both boastful and conceited. But he has got some good qualities, has Toady…if you look hard!

And with that Mole got into the boat and took the sculls, while the Rat settled himself comfortably in the stern, and the friends set off down the river.

Rat: There's Toad Hall. That's the Banqueting-hall you're looking at now—very old, that is. Toad is rather rich, you know, and this is really one of the nicest houses in these parts though we never admit as much to Toad.

They disembarked, and strolled across the gay flower-decked lawns in search of Toad, whom they found resting in a wicker garden-chair, with a pre-occupied expression of face, and a large map spread out on his knees.

Rat: Busy as always, I see, Toad. This is my friend, Moley.

Toad:(exuberant) How *kind* of both of you to visit! And what a coincidence. I was just going to send a boat down the river for you, Ratty, with strict orders that you were to be fetched up here at once, whatever you were doing. Come inside and have something! You don't know how lucky it is, your turning up just now

Rat: Settle down, Toady!

Mole: It's a delightful residence, Mr Toad.

Toad: Finest house on the whole river. Or anywhere else, for that matter. Now as it happens, you are the very animals I wanted. You've got to help me. It's most important!

Rat: It's about your rowing, I expect.

Toad: Oh, pooh to boating! Silly boyish amusement. I've given that up *long* ago. Sheer waste of time, that's what it is. No, I've discovered the real thing, the only genuine occupation for a lifetime. I propose to devote the remainder of mine to it, and can only regret the wasted years that lie behind me, squandered in trivialities. Come with me to the stable yard, dear Ratty, and you too Moley, and you'll see what I mean!

He led the way to the stable and there, drawn out of the coach-house into the open, they saw a caravan, shining with newness, painted a canary-yellow with green and red wheels.

Toad: There you are! There's real life for you, embodied in that little cart. The open road, the dusty highway, the heath, the common, the hedgerows, the rolling downs! Here to-day, up and off to somewhere else to-morrow! The whole world before you…

Mole: *(excited)* Oh my, oh my. It's wonderful, Ratty.

Rat: *(scoffing)* It's a caravan, that's all it is!

Mole: Oh it's so much more. There are little sleeping bunks and a little table that's folded up against the wall. And there is a cooking-stove and lockers and book-shelves and a bird-cage with a bird in it! Wonderful, just wonderful.

Toad: Pots, pans, jugs, and kettles of every size. You see, all complete...you'll find that nothing whatever has been forgotten, when we make our start this afternoon.

Rat: *(shocked)* I beg your pardon...what do you mean *'we,'* and *'start,'* and *'this afternoon'*?

Toad: Now, dear good old Ratty, you've *got* to come. I can't possibly manage without you, I want to show you the world! Show you both!

Mole: *(very excited)* Wonderful, wonderful!

Rat: I don't care. I'm not coming. I'm going to stick to my old river... and what's more, Mole's going to stick to me and do as I do, aren't you, Mole?

Mole: I am? *(Then without conviction)* Of course I am. I'll always stick to you, Ratty. *(Pause)* All the same, it sounds as if it might have been—well, rather fun, you know!

The Rat saw the look of disappointment on his friend's face and he was such a good soul that his resolve wavered. He really did hate disappointing people....

Rat: I don't know… I suppose we could…

Toad: Can you imagine the joy of the open roads? The colours of the flowers, the songs of the birds. And all the characters we will meet. Animals you'd never see on the river.

Mole: Oh that would be a real adventure….wouldn't it, Ratty?

And before he could answer, it was taken for granted that the trip was a settled thing.

When they were quite ready, the now triumphant Toad led his companions to the paddock to capture the old grey horse, who, without having been consulted, and to his extreme annoyance, had been assigned the dustiest job in this dusty expedition.

Transition

It was a golden afternoon. The smell of the dust they kicked up was rich and satisfying; out of thick orchards on either side the road, birds called and whistled to them cheerily; good-natured wayfarers, passing, gave them a "Good day," or stopped to say nice things about their beautiful cart; and rabbits, sitting at their front doors in the hedgerows, held up their fore-paws, and said, "Oh my! Oh my! Oh my!"

Late in the evening, tired and happy and miles from home, they stopped on a remote common far from habitations and ate their simple supper sitting on the grass by the side of the cart.

Toad: Will you look at that moon, fellows? And all the stars. This is the real life for gentlemen. All that talk about your old river, Ratty, when we have this waiting for us. *(Yawns)*. Well, it's time for me to say goodnight. *(Yawns again)* Such adventures awaiting us tomorrow.

(Pause, followed by a soft snore)

Rat: *(annoyed, but speaking softly)* My river! I *don't* talk about my river. But I *think* about it. I think about it—all the time!

Mole: *(quietly)* I'll do whatever you like, Ratty. Shall we run away to-morrow morning, *very* early and go back to our dear old hole on the river?

Rat: No, no, we'll see it out. We ought to stick by Toad till this trip is ended. It wouldn't be safe for him to be left to himself. It won't take very long. His fads never do. Time for some sleep. Good night, Moley.

Mole: Good night, dear Ratty.

After so much open air and excitement Toad slept very soundly, and no amount of shaking could rouse him out of bed next morning. So the Mole and Ratty set about making things right for the day. Ratty saw to the horse, and lit a fire, and cleaned last night's cups and plates, ready for breakfast, while Mole trudged off to the nearest village, a long way off, for milk and eggs and the various necessaries the Toad had, of course, forgotten to provide.

The hard work had all been done, and the two animals were resting, thoroughly exhausted, by the time Toad appeared on the scene, fresh and gay.

Toad: What a wonderful day. And such an pleasant life we're leading now with none of those worries and fatigues of housekeeping at home. Come on, you two lazybones. We can't spend all day lounging round the fire.

They were strolling along the high-road, Mole by the horse's head, talking to him, since the horse had complained that he was being frightfully left out of it; the Toad and Ratty walking behind the cart talking together — at least Toad was talking, and Rat was saying at intervals...

Rat: *(uninterested)* Yes, precisely; and what did you say to him?

...and thinking all the time of something very different, when far behind them they heard a faint hum, like the drone of a distant bee. Glancing back, they saw a small cloud of dust, with a dark centre, advancing at incredible speed, while from out of the dust a sound emerged, like roar of a wild animal.

(<u>SFX</u>: Sound of an old fashion car engine)

Mole: *(distressed)* What is it?

Rat: Monster!

Toad: *(impressed)* Oh my, oh my. It's wonderful.

He had caught a glimpse of a magnificent motor-car - immense, breath-snatching, passionate, with its pilot tense and hugging the wheel - that seemed to possess all earth and air. It flung up a cloud of dust that wrapped around the three travellers, as it passed and then, in a moment, it was gone. All that was left was a dwindling speck in the far distance.

Rat: *(angry, shouting)* You villains!

Mole: Oh dear. They have scared the Horse. He's run away. And look what's happened to our lovely caravan. It's fallen in the ditch and the wheels and doors have come off.

Rat: *(still angry)* You scoundrels, you highwaymen, you—you—road-hogs!—I'll have the law of you! Toad? Don't you have anything to say. They've wrecked your caravan.

Toad: *(to himself)* Vrooom, vroom…

Rat: What?

Toad: *(increasingly excited)* Glorious, stirring sight! The poetry in motion! The *real* way to travel! The *only* way to travel! Villages skipped, towns and cities jumped—always somebody else's horizon! Vroom, vroom.

Rat: Oh *stop* being an ass, Toad! Come over here and give us a hand with the caravan.

Toad: And to think I never *knew*! All those wasted years that lie behind me, I never knew, never even *dreamt*! But *now*—but now that I know…that I fully realise! Oh what a track lies before me. What dust-clouds shall spring up behind me

Mole: What are we to do with him, Ratty? He's seems quite mad.

Rat: Nothing at all. There is really nothing to be done. You see, I've known him a long time. He is now possessed. He'll continue like that for days, like an animal walking in a happy dream, quite useless for all practical purposes. Never mind him. Let's see what to be done with the cart.

Mole: I don't think there is anything to be done with it. The wheels have fallen off.

Rat: Oh well, I suppose we'll go to the railway station then, and with some luck we may pick up a train that'll get us back to river to-night.

Mole: And what shall we do with Mr Toad?

Toad: *(dreamily)* Vroom, vroom.

And so, Mole and Ratty caught a train that took them back to the beloved hole in the riverbank, with Ratty swearing he'd never leave the river again, while Toad went to town the very next morning and ordered …a large and very expensive motor-car!

Transition

This is where we meet Badger. Kind old Badger. Wise old Badger. Wonderful old…

Badger: Stop saying old …

Rat: You're always grumpy when you're hungry, Badger.

Badger: I'm not grumpy! *(Pause)* But I am hungry. Is there any dinner?

Rat: That's why we invited you, old chap…that and to talk about our friend Toad.

Mole: I'm so glad to finally meet you, Mr Badger. I will get you some bread and jam right away.

Otter: Perhaps a little something more for me as well, Moley. I'm still quite hungry.

Mole: I think you are always hungry.

Rat: What are you doing here, Otter?

Otter: You invited me. Come and have dinner any time, you said.

Rat: I never did.

Otter: We'll, it was implied.

Mole: Here, I've brought enough for everyone.

Badger: *(eating)* Ummm... aaaah... *(with mouth full)* ...So what's this about Toad.

Rat: Oh, he's gone from bad to worse. Another smash-up only last week, and a bad one. You see, he will insist on driving himself, and he's hopelessly incapable. He's convinced he's a natural-born driver, and nobody can teach him anything.

Badger: How many has he had?

Rat: Smashes, or machines? I suppose it's the same thing—with Toad. This is the seventh. You know that coach-house of his? Well, it's piled up—literally piled up to the roof—with fragments of motor-cars, none of them bigger than your hat!

Mole: *(mouth full)* He's been in hospital three times, and as for the fines he's had to pay...it's simply awful to think of.

Rat: He'll be killed or bankrupt— one of the two, sooner or later. *(Pause)* Badger! we're his friends— we should do something.

Otter: Is there any more toast...and butter...and yes, more jam.

Mole: Are you ever full, Otter?

Otter: I suppose I will be … one day. But it is really quite difficult being an Otter. We are always hungry … I don't know why …we just are and people think we are greedy. But we're not. It's just our nature and you can't do anything about your nature, can you? I say, are you going to eat that roll, Mole?

Badger: *(solemn and loud)* The hour has come!

Mole: *(jumping in surprise)* Oh my…

Rat: What hour?

Badger: *Whose* hour?   That is the question.   Toad's hour!   You are right Ratty. We are his friends and it's time we put a stop to all this nonsense.

Mole: Hooray! *We'll* teach him to be a sensible Toad!

Otter: *(eating, mouth full)* I've heard he has another car being delivered to Toad Hall today. Exceptionally powerful, they say.

Rat: Then there is no time to waste. At this very moment Toad will be busy arraying himself in those singularly hideous driving clothes he wears and that ridiculous scarf.

Badger: Right you are! We'll rescue the poor animal! We'll convert him!

Mole: *(gaily)* He'll be the most converted Toad that ever was before we've done with him! Otter, are you coming with us? It'll be quite an adventure.

Otter: Would like to chaps. I mean Toad's a grand fellow and all that, well worth saving which you can't say about everyone. But Mrs Otter will have the dinner on and… well, you know…

So the brave Band of Three - Mole, Ratty and Badger - set off on their mission of mercy and reached the carriage-drive of Toad Hall to find a shiny new motor-car standing in front of the house. As they neared the front door it was flung open, and Mr. Toad, arrayed in goggles, cap, enormous overcoat and that ridiculous scarf, came swaggering down the steps, drawing on his gauntleted gloves.

Toad: Hullo, fellows! You're just in time to come with me for a jolly drive in the country…to come for a jolly…for a—er—jolly… What's the problem? You don't look very happy at all.

Badger: Take him inside.

Toad: What are you doing? Let go of me.

Rat: I'm afraid you won't be going anywhere to-day, Toad.

Toad: I will!

Badger: First of all, take those ridiculous things off!

Toad: Shan't! It's my driving outfit. I have just bought this scarf.

Badger: Then we'll take them off for you.

Toad: What is the meaning of this gross outrage? I demand an instant explanation. What are you doing, Mole?

Mole: I'm so sorry, Mr Toad. But it really is for your own good.

Rat: Stop wriggling around, Toad. It'll go much easier if you're still.

Toad: Let go of me!

They had to lay Toad out on the floor, kicking and calling all sorts of names, before they could get to work properly. Then Ratty sat on him, and the Mole got his motor-clothes off bit by bit. A good deal of his blustering spirit seemed to evaporate with the removal of his fine panoply. He became merely Toad, no longer the Terror of the Highway, and he giggled feebly.

Badger: You knew it would come to this, sooner or later, Toad. You've disregarded all the warnings we've given you, you've gone on squandering the money your father left you, and you're giving us animals a bad name in the district by your furious driving and your smashes and your rows with the police.

Toad: *(obsequiously)* I meant no harm, Badger, but you know I've have always been an independent sort.

Badger: Independence is all very well, but we animals never allow our friends to make fools of themselves. Now, you're a good fellow in many respects, so I'll make one more effort to help you see reason. You will come with me into the smoking-room, and there you will hear some facts about yourself; and we'll see whether you come out of that room the same Toad that you went in.

And with that he took Toad firmly by the arm, led him into the smoking-room, and closed the door behind them.

Rat: *(contemptuous)* Really…what's the point of that?

Mole: Perhaps it will work, Ratty. I mean, Badger is very convincing.

Rat: *Talking* to Toad'll never cure him. He'll *say* anything and then do the opposite.

After some three-quarters of an hour the door opened, and the Badger reappeared, solemnly followed by a very limp and dejected Toad.

Badger: Sit down there, Toad.

Toad: *(deflated)* I will, Badger. I'll sit and not move …

Badger: And think about all we've discussed.

Toad: …and think about all we've discussed…

Badger: Well, my friends, I'm pleased to inform you that Toad has at last seen the error of his ways. He is truly sorry for his misguided conduct in the past…

Toad: *(interrupting quietly)* …truly sorry…

Badger: *(annoyed by the interruption)* Yes! ….and he has undertaken to give up motor-cars entirely and forever. I have his solemn promise to that effect.

Toad: Solemn promise.

Mole: That is very good news…

Rat: *(dubious)* Very good news indeed, if only—*if* only—

Badger: There's only one thing more to be done. Toad, I want you to repeat, before your friends here, what you fully admitted to me in the smoking-room just now. First, you are sorry for what you've done, and you see the folly of your ways?

(Long Pause)

Badger: Toad, did you hear me…?

(Long pause)

Badger: Toad?

Toad: *(defiantly)* No! I'm *not* sorry. And it wasn't folly at all! It was simply glorious!

Badger: What? You backsliding animal, didn't you tell me just now, in there—

Toad: Oh, yes, yes, in *there*, I'd have said anything in *there*.

Rat: I told you so!

Toad: *(appeasing)* You're so eloquent, dear Badger, and so moving, and so convincing, and put all your points so frightfully well—you can do what you like with me in *there*, and you know it. But I've been searching my mind since, and going over things in it, and I find that I'm not a bit sorry or repentant really, so it's no earthly good saying I am; now, is it?

Badger: Then you don't promise not to touch a motor-car again?

Toad: Certainly not! On the contrary, I faithfully promise that the very first motor-car I see, *vroom vroom* off I go…

Badger: Very well, then. Take him upstairs chaps, and lock him in his bedroom. He'll stay there until he's fully over this nonsense.

Toad: Unhand me!

Rat: It's for your own good, Toady, you know it is. Think what fun we shall have together when you've quite got over this!

Mole: We'll take great care of everything for you till you're well, Mr Toad.

Toad: Let me go. You traitors! You villains! You…you…weasels!

(<u>SFX</u>: Door slamming shut)

Toad: *(muffled)* Cowards! Villains! Let me out.

Mole: Oh dear. He's very upset.

Rat: Yes, it's going to be a tedious business. I've never seen Toad so determined.

Badger: He must never be unguarded for a moment. We shall have to take it in turns to be with him, till the poison has worked itself out of his system.

They arranged watches accordingly. Each animal took it in turns to sleep in Toad's room at night, and they divided the day up between them. At first, Toad was undoubtedly very trying to his careful guardians. He would arrange bedroom chairs in the form of a motor-car and crouch on the foremost of them, bend forward and staring fixedly ahead, make uncouth and ghastly noises....

Toad: Vroom Vroom

...that grew ever louder

Toad: *(louder)* Vroom Vroom

...until the climax was reached

Toad: *(loud)* VROOM VROOM

... and he'd turned a complete somersault, and lay prostrate on the floor.

As time passed, however, these painful seizures grew gradually less frequent until finally one fine morning Ratty, whose turn it was to be on duty, went upstairs to relieve Badger, who he found fidgeting and anxious to be off on a long ramble round his wood.

Badger: Toad's still in bed. Can't get much out of him, except, 'Oh leave me alone, I don't want anything'... Now, you look out, Rat! When Toad's quiet and submissive, he's at his worst. There's sure to be something up. I know him.

(<u>SFX</u>: Door closing)

Rat: How are you to-day, old chap?

Toad: *(feebly)* Thank you so much, dear Ratty! So good of you to ask! But first tell me how you are yourself, and the excellent Mole?

Rat: Oh, *we're* all right. Mole is going out for a walk with Badger. They'll be out till lunch time, so you and I will spend a pleasant morning together, and I'll do my best to amuse you. Now jump up, there's a good fellow, and don't mope around on a fine morning like this!

Toad: Dear, kind Rat, how little you understand of my condition, and how very far I am from 'jumping up' now—if ever! But do not trouble yourself about me. I hate being a burden to my friends, and I do not expect to be one much longer. Indeed, I almost hope not.

Rat: Well, I hope not, too! You've been a fine bother to us all this time, and I'm glad to hear it's going to stop. With weather like this, and the boating season just beginning…it's not the trouble we mind, but what you're making us miss.

Toad: I'm afraid it *is* the trouble you mind, though. I can quite understand it. It's natural enough. You're tired of bothering about me. I mustn't ask you to do anything further. I'm a nuisance, I know.

Rat: You are, indeed. But I tell you, I'd take any trouble on earth for you, if only you'd be a sensible animal.

Toad: If I thought that, Ratty, then I would beg you—for the last time, probably—to step round to the village as quickly as possible—even now it may be too late—and fetch the doctor. But don't you bother. It's only a trouble, and perhaps we may as well let things take their course.

Rat: What do you want a doctor for?

Toad: Surely you have noticed of late…But, no—why should you? Noticing things is only a trouble. To-morrow, indeed, you may be saying to yourself, 'Oh, if only I had noticed sooner! If only I had done something!' But no; it's a trouble. Never mind—forget that I asked.

Rat: *(alarmed)* Look here, old man, of course I'll fetch a doctor for you, if you really think you need him. But you can hardly be bad enough for that yet. Let's talk about something else.

Toad: I fear, dear friend, that 'talk' can do little in a case like this—or doctors either, for that matter; still, one must grasp at the slightest straw. And, by the way—while you are about it—I *hate* to give you additional trouble, but I happen to remember that you will pass the lawyer's office —would you mind asking him to come as well? It would be a convenience to me, and there are moments—perhaps I should say there is *a* moment—when one must face disagreeable tasks!

"A lawyer! Oh, he must be really bad! Ratty thought, as he hurried from the room, not forgetting, however, to lock the door carefully behind him.

Outside, he stopped to consider. The other two were far away, and he had no one to consult.

Rat: *(to himself)* It's best to be on the safe side. I've known Toad fancy himself frightfully bad before, without the slightest reason; but I've never heard him ask for a lawyer! If there's nothing really the matter, the doctor will tell him he's an old ass, and cheer him up; and that will be something gained. I'd better humour him and go; it won't take very long.

As Ratty headed off to the village on his errand of mercy, Toad, who had hopped lightly out of bed as soon as he heard the key turned in the lock, watched him eagerly from the window till he disappeared down the carriage-drive.

Toad: Off you go, Ratty. Ha. Think you can keep Toad locked up. Not likely.

Then, laughing heartily, he dressed as quickly as possible in the smartest suit he could lay hands on, filled his pockets with cash which he took from a small drawer in the dressing-table, and knotting the sheets from his bed together climbed out the bedroom window.

Rat: Oh dear

It was a gloomy lunch for Ratty when Badger and Mole returned.

Badger: You've been a bit of a duffer this time!

Rat: *(pathetic)* I know…

Badger: Fooled by Toad…of all animals.

Rat: *(weakly)* He did it awfully well.

Badger: He did *you* awfully well!

Mole: What shall we do, Mr Badger. We must find him.

Badger: Find him where, Mole? He's got clear away and the worst of it is, he'll be so conceited with what he'll think is his cleverness that he may commit any folly.

Rat: Well one small comfort is we're free now and needn't waste any more of our precious time on sentry duty.

Badger: That may be so, but we'd better continue to sleep at Toad Hall for a while longer. Toad is sure to be brought back at any moment *(beat)*…on a stretcher, or between two policemen.

At that very moment, Toad, gay and irresponsible, was walking briskly along the high road, some miles from his home. At first he had taken by-paths, and crossed many fields, and changed his course several times, in case of pursuit; but now, feeling safe from recapture, and the sun smiling brightly on him, and all Nature joining in a chorus of approval to the song of self-praise that his own heart was singing, he almost danced along the road in his satisfaction and conceit.

Toad: *(to himself)* Smart piece of work that! Brain against brute force—and brain came out on the top—as it's bound to do. Poor old Ratty! My! won't he catch it when the Badger gets back! A worthy fellow, Ratty, with many good qualities, but very little intelligence and absolutely no education. I must take him in hand some day, and see if I can make something of him. *(Pause)* What's that sign say…The Red Lion! What luck. I'm sure they'll have meals and I'm absolutely starving …coming up with a great escape will do that to you…

He was about half-way through his meal when a familiar sound made him start and tremble all over.

(<u>SFX</u>: Vintage motor car engine)

Toad: *(overwhelmed with excitement)* Oh my. Oh my…vroom, vroom…

Presently a party entered, talking loudly about their experiences of the morning and the merits of the chariot that had carried them there. Toad listened eagerly, all ears, for a time; at last he could stand it no longer. He slipped out of the room quietly, paid his bill at the bar, and as soon as he got outside sauntered round quietly to the inn-yard.

Toad: *(to himself)* There cannot be any harm, in my only just *looking* at it!

The car stood in the middle of the yard, quite unattended. Toad walked slowly round it, inspecting, criticising, musing deeply.

Toad: I wonder…I wonder if this sort of car *starts* easily?

Next moment, hardly knowing how it came about, he found he had hold of the handle and was turning it. As the familiar sound broke forth, the old passion seized Toad and completely mastered him, body and soul. As if in a dream he found himself, somehow, in the driver's seat; as if in a dream, he pulled the lever and swung the car round the yard and out through the archway; and, as if in a dream, all sense of right and wrong, all fear of obvious consequences, seemed temporarily suspended. He increased his pace, and the car devoured the street and leapt forth on the high road through the open country.

Toad: Yippee. I am Toad once more! Toad at his best and highest. Toad the terror, the traffic-queller, the Lord of the lone trail, before whom all must give way or be smitten into nothingness and everlasting night

(SFX: Sound of a magistrate's gavel)

Magistrate: Quiet…quiet in the court. *(Pause)* To my mind, the *only* difficulty that presents itself in this otherwise very clear case is, how we can possibly make it sufficiently hot for the incorrigible rogue and hardened ruffian whom we see cowering in the dock before us. Let me see: he has been found guilty, on the clearest evidence, first, of stealing a valuable motor-car; secondly, of driving to the public danger; and, thirdly, of gross impertinence to the rural police. Now I must consider, what is the very stiffest penalty the court can impose for each of these offences? Some people would consider, that stealing the motor-car was the worst offence; and so it is. But cheeking the police undoubtedly carries the severest penalty; and so it ought. Supposing I was to say twelve months for the theft, which is mild; and three years for the furious driving, which is lenient; and fifteen years for the cheek, which was pretty bad sort of cheek, judging by what we've heard from the witness-box, even if you only believe one-tenth part of what you heard, and I never believe more myself—those figures, if added together correctly, tot up to nineteen years— *(Pause)* Let's make it a round twenty years and be on the safe side!

(SFX: Bangs gavel again)

Magistrate: Prisoner! Pull yourself together and try and stand up straight. It's going to be twenty years for you this time. And mind, if you appear before me again, upon any charge whatever, I shall have to deal with you very seriously!

The rusty key creaked in the lock, the great door clanged behind him…

… and Toad found himself a helpless prisoner in the remotest dungeon of the best-guarded keep of the stoutest castle in all the length and breadth of the land.

(SFX: Heavy Gaol door slamming shut)

Toad: Oh dear …

Transition

Toad sat in a dark and dank dungeon and thought about the damp walls of the medieval fortress that separated him from the outer world of sunshine and high roads...

Toad: This is the end of everything or at least the end of Toad, which is the same thing. Popular and handsome Toad, rich and hospitable Toad, Toad so free and careless and debonair! *(Loudly to the room)* Why has this happened to me? Why have I been imprisoned for stealing such a handsome motor-car. I mean it was not my fault, who could resist all that soft leather and shiny silver? *(Beat, then quietly to himself)* Vroom, vroom. *(Thoughtful pause)* And years for offering fat, red-faced policemen the benefit of my opinion! It's so unfair, so cruel, so...stupid! *(Sobs)*

With lamentations such as these he passed his days and nights for several weeks, refusing his meals or intermediate light refreshments, though the grim and ancient gaoler, knowing that Toad's pockets were well lined, frequently pointed out that many comforts, and indeed luxuries, could by arrangement be sent in — at a price — from outside.

Now, as it happened, the gaoler had a daughter - a pleasant girl and good-hearted, who assisted her father in the lighter duties of his post. She was particularly fond of animals and this kind young girl pitied Toad and told her father that she couldn't bear seeing him so unhappy.

Daughter: Let me look after him and soon he won't be so thin. You know how fond of animals I am. I'll have him eating from my hand…and doing all sorts of things, before you know it.

Gaoler: Do what you like, you usually do! Truth is I'm quite tired of that Toad. His sulks and his airs and his meanness. You should hear the names he calls me. Terrible they are…very hurtful indeed and all I'm doing is my duty … I've met nicer murderers, I have…

So off she went on her errand of mercy and found the Toad lying despondent on his cot.

Daughter: Cheer up, Toad! Sit up and be a sensible animal. And do try and eat a bit of dinner. See, I've brought you some of mine, hot from the oven!

Toad: Ummmm…what's that delicious smell. Cabbage? Is it cabbage?

Daughter: It's bubble and squeak. Here, try a mouthful.

Toad: Well…perhaps just a spoon…*(Pause, then firmly)* No, I will not! I am miserable and the miserable do not eat. Take it away!

Daughter: If you insist. But I will come back to see you this afternoon.

Toad: Do as you please. The circumstances will not have changed and I will not be tempted out of misery by some delicious smells…

But that is exactly what happened. The girl returned with a tray bearing a cup of fragrant tea; and a plate piled up with hot buttered toast, cut thick, very brown on both sides, with the butter running through the holes in it in great golden drops, like honey from the honeycomb.

Toad: Oh, this reminds me of so many things. Warm kitchens and breakfasts on bright frosty mornings. Of cosy parlour firesides on winter evenings, when one's ramble was over, and slippered feet. *(Groaning sadly)* Oh, Toad Hall. How I miss it…and all my friends.

Daughter: Tell me about Toad Hall. It sounds beautiful.

Toad: Well... *(in a formal voice)* Toad Hall, is an eligible, self-contained gentleman's residence, very unique; dating in part from the fourteenth century, but replete with every modern convenience. Up-to-date sanitation. Five minutes from church, post-office, and golf-links. Suitable for—

Daughter: *(laughing)* Bless me...I don't want to *buy* it. Tell me something *real* about it.

Toad: Ofcourse, something real...but first, can I trouble you for some more tea and toast?

Through mouthfuls of toast and between slurps of tea, he told her about the Boat House, and the fish-pond, and the old walled kitchen-garden; and about the pig-styes and the stables, and the pigeon-house and the hen-house; and about the dairy, and the wash-house, and the china-cupboards, and the linen-presses (she liked that bit especially); and about the Banqueting Hall, and the fun they had there when the other animals were gathered round the table and Toad was at his best, singing songs, telling stories, carrying on generally. On and on he talked, so much that by the time she said good-night, Toad was very much the same sanguine, self-satisfied animal that he had been of old.

Transition

One morning the girl was very thoughtful and it seemed to Toad that she was not paying proper attention to his witty sayings and sparkling comments.

Daughter: Toad, I have an aunt who is a washerwoman.

Toad: There, there, never mind; think no more about it. *I* have several aunts who *ought* to be washerwomen.

Daughter: Do be quiet a minute! You talk too much, that's your chief fault, and I'm trying to think, and you hurt my head. As I said, I have an aunt who is a washerwoman; she does the washing for all the prisoners in this castle—we try to keep any paying business of that sort in the family, you understand. She takes out the washing on Monday morning, and brings it in on Friday evening. This is a Thursday. Now, this is what occurs to me: you're very rich and she's very poor. A few pounds wouldn't make any difference to you, and it would mean a lot to her. I think if she were properly approached you could come to some arrangement by which she would let you have her dress and bonnet and you could escape from the castle as the official washerwoman. You're very alike in many respects—particularly about the figure.

Toad: *(offended)* We're *not!* I have a very elegant figure…for what I am.

Daughter: *(angry)* So has my aunt, for what *she* is! But have it your own way, you horrid, proud, ungrateful animal. I was just feeling sorry for you, and trying to help…

Toad: Yes, yes, I understand…But surely you wouldn't have Mr. Toad of Toad Hall, going about the country disguised as a washerwoman!

Daughter: Then you can stop here!

Toad: Well…I suppose if no one knew…I mean it could be our little secret, after all. Ours and your aunt, of course…

Daughter: Sensible Toad! Tomorrow evening, I will bring you her clothes, a cotton gown and shawl…and a rusty black bonnet, I think…

The following evening, good as her word, the gaoler's daughter brought the cotton gown and shawl and rusty black bonnet and proceeded to "hook-and-eye" him into the elaborate disguise.

Daughter: Let me fold this shawl over your shoulders…there I think that's right. Now for the bonnet.

Toad: Be careful. Don't tie those strings so tight

Daughter: Do you want it to blow off while your passing a guard? There, how's that. *(Pause)* I've tied my aunt up and left her in the washroom. That was our agreement. This way she can say she was a victim of the notorious Toad *(laughs)*. Finished!

Toad: How do I look?

Daughter: You're the very image of her! I'm sure you never looked so respectable in all your life. Now, good-bye, Toad, and good luck. Go straight down the way you came up; and if any one says anything to you, remember you're a widow woman, quite alone in the world and grunt something miserable…you should be good at that.

With a quaking heart, Toad set forth sure he'd be caught at any moment but the washerwoman's squat figure in its familiar cotton print seemed a passport through every barred door and grim gateway. After what seemed like hours he exited the last gate and stood in a field, dizzy from the smells of the countryside and the sound of the wind whistling through the branches.

Toad: FREEDOM!!

ACT TWO

Toad started to walk towards the lights of the town, wondering what he would do next, when his attention was caught by some red and green lights a little way off and the sound of puffing and snorting...

Toad: Aha! this is a piece of luck! A train is just the thing I need; and what's more, I won't need go through the town to get it. Imagine if I were caught in this ridiculous disguise. Toad was dressed as a washerwoman, they'd say. Toad of Toad Hall, would be Toad of the Laundry. Humiliating...

He made his way to the station, consulted a time-table, and found that a train, bound more or less in the direction of his home, was due to pass through in half-an-hour.

Toad: What splendid luck. I shall be in Toad Hall, sitting at the fireside, by evening.

But luck failed him when he went to purchase his ticket and reached for the money tucked into his waist coat pocket. There was no pocket...

Toad: Look here! I find I've left my purse behind. Just give me that ticket, will you, and I'll send the money on to-morrow? I'm well-known in these parts.

But the clerk just told him to stop holding up the line and full of despair, Toad wandered blindly down the platform where the train was standing...

Toad: It's so hard. I am within sight of safety only to be baulked by the want of a few wretched shillings. Very soon my escape will be discovered, the hunt will be on *(sobs)* and if I'm caught, I'll be loaded with chains, dragged back again to prison and put on bread-and-water!

Engine Driver: Hullo, mother! what's the trouble? You don't look particularly cheerful.

Toad: *(to himself)* What? Oh, it's the engine driver *(speaking as the washerwoman)* Oh, sir! I am a poor unhappy washerwoman, and I've lost all my money, and can't pay for a ticket, and I *must* get home to-night somehow, and whatever I am to do I don't know. Oh dear, Oh dear!

Engine Driver: That's a bad business, indeed. Lost your money—and can't get home—and got some kids, too, waiting for you, I dare say?

Toad: Any amount of 'em. And they'll be hungry—and playing with matches—and upsetting lamps, the little innocents!—and quarrelling, and going on generally. Oh dear, Oh dear!

Engine Driver: Well, I'll tell you what I'll do. You're a washerwoman by your trade, says you. Very well, that's that. And I'm an engine-driver, as you see, and there's no denying it's terribly dirty work. Uses up a power of shirts, it does, till my missus is fair tired of washing of 'em. If you'll wash a few shirts for me when you get home, and send 'em along, I'll give you a ride on my engine. It's against the Company's regulations, but we're not so very particular in these out-of-the-way parts.

Toad: *(quietly to himself)* What will I do? I've never washed a shirt in my life and couldn't if I tried.

Engine Driver: Well what say you mother? Do we have a bargain?

Toad: *(still quietly to himself)* When I get safely home to Toad Hall, and have money again, and pockets to put it in, I can send him enough to pay for all his washing, and perhaps some shirts too. His wife will be ever so grateful, I'm sure. *(In the washerwoman's voice)*. Yes, we have a deal, sir!

And on he climbed, standing next to the Engine Driver as the train left the station.

Toad: *(in Toad's voice)* Woah, look at all those fields, and trees, and hedges, and cows, and horses…I'm free and I'll be having my tea in Toad Hall tonight.

Engine Driver: What's that?

Toad: *(washerwoman's voice)* Oh sir, I was just saying how lovely the countryside is …and how kind you are to take me…

Engine Driver: *(cutting Toad off)* That's strange; we're the last train running in this direction to-night, yet I could swear I hear another following us! *(Longish pause)* There, I can see it clearly now! It is an engine, on our rails, coming along at a great pace! It looks as if we're being pursued!

Toad: *(alarmed)* Pursued? Oh dear. Oh dear.

Engine Driver: And they're gaining on us fast! *(Pause)* It's very odd. The engine is crowded with the queerest lot of people, I ever seen! Men like ancient warders and policemen in their helmets, waving truncheons;

Toad: Truncheons! Oh dear.

Engine driver: …and there's some shabbily dressed men in pot-hats…with revolvers and walking-sticks.

Toad: Revolvers. Oh no…

Engine driver: They're all shouting 'Stop, stop, stop!. That's a queer thing…why would they want that…

Toad: *(in his own voice)* Save me, please save me, dear kind Mr. Engine-driver, and I will confess everything!

Engine driver: Confess? What do you have to confess, mother?

Toad: I am not the simple washerwoman I seem to be! I have no children waiting for me, innocent or otherwise! *(Throwing off the shawl)* I am Toad—the well-known and popular Mr. Toad. And I have just escaped, by my great daring and cleverness, from a loathsome dungeon into which my enemies had flung me; and if those fellows on that engine recapture me, it will be chains and bread-and-water and straw and misery once more for poor, unhappy, innocent Toad!

Engine Driver: Toad, you say? Well I would never have guessed. You have the shape of a washerwoman. What were you put in prison for?

Toad: Nothing much. A mistake really. I borrowed a motor-car while the owners were at lunch; they had no need of it at the time. However, the police called it theft and magistrates take such a harsh view on such things…

Engine Driver: Borrowed a motor car? That's what you call it.. You are a thoroughly wicked toad, and by rights I ought to give you up…

Toad: *(pathetically)* Oh please, have mercy on me... You'd find I'm quite a decent fellow once I'm out of this dress!

Engine Driver: *(wavering)* Well...you are evidently in sore trouble...

Toad: I am! And all over a misunderstanding...

Engine Driver: Alright, I will not give you up. I don't hold with motor-cars, for one thing; and I don't hold with being ordered about by policemen when I'm on my own engine, for another. And the sight of an animal in tears always makes me feel queer and soft-hearted. So cheer up, Toad! I'll do my best, and we may beat them yet!

And with that, they both piled on more coals, shovelling furiously; the furnace roared, the sparks flew, the engine leapt and swung, but still their pursuers slowly gained.

Engine Driver: I'm afraid it's no good, Toad. You see, they are running light, and they have the better engine. There's just one thing left for us to do, and it's your only chance. A short way ahead of us is a long tunnel, and on the other side of that the line passes through a thick wood. Now, I will put on all the speed I can while we are running through the tunnel, but the other fellows will slow down a bit, naturally, for fear of an accident. When we are through, I will shut off steam and put on brakes as hard as I can, and the moment it's safe to do so you must jump and hide in the wood. Then I will go full speed ahead again, and they will chase me! Now be ready to jump when I tell you!

So more coals were piled on as the train raced into the tunnel, and the engine rushed and roared and rattled, till at last they shot out the other end into fresh air and peaceful moonlight, and saw the wood lying dark and helpful upon either side of the line.

(SFX: Train braking)

Engine Driver: Now, jump!

Toad: I think…I'm sure we are still going to fast.

Engine Driver: Jump I said, you cowardly toad!

Toad: Aaaargh.

Toad rolled down the embankment and at the bottom picked himself up unhurt. He stood for a moment quite angry at being pushed, but then watching the second train speed by he gave a hearty laugh.

Toad: Capture Toad? Not likely! *(Pause)* I'M FREE! And I shall soon be walking into Toad Hall in triumph. There will be hoorahs and cheers of welcome home. All I need to do is set off.

And set off he did, singing his praises to the fields and the hills as he walked.

Toad: Ho, ho! what a clever Toad I am! There is surely no animal equal to me for cleverness in the whole world! My enemies shut me up in prison. Encircled by sentries, watched night and day by warders; I walk out through them all. They pursue me with engines and policemen and revolvers, I snap my fingers at them and vanish, laughing, into space. Ho, ho! I am The Toad, the handsome, the popular, the successful Toad!

After some miles of country lanes he reached the high road and as he turned into it and glanced along its length, he saw approaching him a speck that turned into a dot ...

Toad: *(quietly)* Vroom vroom?

and then into a blob…

Toad: *(louder)* Vroom, vroom.

…and then into something very familiar…

Toad: *(loud, excited)* VROOM VROOM.

He watched the motor car come along at an easy pace and stepped confidently to wave down his brothers of the wheel.

(SFX: Sound of a car coming closer)

Toad: *(shouting)* Hallo! You there, could you give me a lift? *(To himself)* Wonderful, they are slowing down. Perhaps I can convince them to let me drive. What a lark it would be to drive up to Toad Hall in a motor car. I can not wait to see the look on Badger's face. *(Pause)* What a wonderful piece of machinery. So shiney, so…*(Shocked)* Oh no. It can't be…

Toad became very pale. His heart turned to water, his knees buckled under him as he doubled up and collapsed with a sickening pain in his stomach, for he saw approaching him the very car he had stolen out of the yard of the Red Lion Hotel!

Toad: *(despairing)* It's all up! It's all over now! Chains and policemen again! Prison again! Dry bread and water again!

The terrible motor-car drew slowly nearer and nearer, till at last it stopped just short of him. Two gentlemen got out and walked round the trembling heap of crumpled misery lying in the road.

Driver 1: Oh dear, this is very sad! Here is a poor old thing fainted on the road

Driver 2: A washerwoman by the look of her... here help me lift her into the car and we'll take her to the hospital.

Driver 1: *(grunting)* My word, she's a heavy one...

Toad: *(to himself, offended)* What's that? Heavy, you say! Well I never! *(Groaning)* Ohhhhh...

Driver 2: You're awake?

Toad:*(washerwoman's voice)* What happened?

Driver 1: You must have been overcome by the heat. You fainted dead away.

Driver 2: You were lying there in the middle of the road, so we stopped to pick you up.

Now fully recovered, Toad smiled a very devious smile.

Toad: Very kind of you, sirs. very kind. My, my this is a magnificent machine. The most magnificent thing I've ever seen. What's it called?

Driver 1: A motor car. You've never seen one?

Toad: I imagine I have …maybe once or twice from afar. Can I sit in the front seat. Just to enjoy the fresh air and view I'd the open road.

And without waiting for an answer he scrambled over the seat and reached out to grab the steering wheel from the hands of the shocked driver. As he did, his scarf and bonnet fell away.

Toad: *(in his own voice)* Vroom, vroom! Washerwoman, indeed! Ho! ho! I am Toad, the motor-car snatcher, the prison-breaker, the Toad who always escapes! Sit still, and you shall know what driving really is…

Toad turned the wheel one way and then another

Driver 2: Watch out!

Driver 1: Grab him!

But Toad was now possessed with the evil spirit of the mechanical monster and could not be stopped. With a half-turn of the wheel Toad sent the car crashing through the low hedge that ran along the roadside and splashing into the horse-pond that lay beyond.

Toad: Aaaargh

Toad found himself flying through the air with the delicate curve of a swallow and was quite enjoying the motion until he landed with a thump on the soft, rich grass of a meadow. Sitting up, he could just see the motor-car in the pond, nearly submerged; the two gentlemen, encumbered by their long coats, were floundering helplessly in the water.

Toad: Ho! ho! Toad again! Toad, as usual, comes out on the top!

And with that he picked himself up and set off running across country as hard as he could, scrambling through hedges, jumping ditches, pounding across fields, until he was so breathless he could only walk a weary walk. That's when he heard something behind him.

Toad: What an *ass* I am! What a *conceited* and heedless ass!

For there behind him, two fields off, were the drivers, still covered in mud and with them was a large policeman, all running towards him as hard as they could go!

Toad: Oh my. Oh dear. Run, Toad! Run, run, run…

He ran as fast as he could, but he really was a fat little animal, and his legs were very short, so they gained on him. Ceasing to heed where he was going, he struggled on blindly and wildly until suddenly the earth failed under his feet and he flew through the air until ….

SPLASH!

Toad: *(spluttering)* I really am quite sick and tired of falling in water… oh my, oh dear…**Wait**…this isn't a pond…

He found himself head over ears in deep water, rapid water, water that bore him along with a force he could not contend with; and he knew that in his blind panic he had run straight into the river!

Toad: *(gasping)* Help! I promise I shall never steal a motor-car again! And I will never sing another conceited song…please, someone one help poor Toad!

But the water pulled him under, swirling him around in its muddy darkness and just when he thought all hope was lost, something reached in and grabbed him.

Toad: *(spluttering, coughing)* What… Hoorah, I'm saved! *(Coughing again)* And who is my hero! I must thank him. He has earned the eternal gratitude of Toad!

Ratty: Hello, Toad!

Toad: *(surprised)* Ratty?

Ratty gripped Toad firmly by the scruff of the neck and hoisted him up onto the bank.

Ratty: Well, a right shambles you look…is that a dress you're wearing.

Toad: Oh Ratty! I've been through such times since I saw you last, you can't imagine! Such trials, such sufferings, and all of which I nobly bore, ofcourse. And then there were such escapes, such disguises, such subterfuges, and all so cleverly planned and carried out! Been in prison—got out of it, of course! Been thrown off a train. Propelled out of a car into the water and then ran into this river. Splash! Splash! Splash! *(Cunningly)* But humbugged them all…*(laughs)*

Rat: Clearly none of it has changed you! Will you stop babbling for a minute so we can change you out of that old cotton? You look like a washerwoman.

Toad: A washerwoman! Yes, that was part of the brilliant plan I…

Rat: Be quiet, Toad. There'll be plenty of time for your bragging when we get back to my hole…

By the time Toad was washed and brushed up, Ratty has lunch on the table. Simple fare, but as usual Toad was hungry and shovelled the food into his mouth, while they he talked and talked about all his adventures, dwelling chiefly on his own cleverness, and presence of mind in emergencies, and cunning in tight places. But the more he talked and boasted, the more grave and silent the Rat became.

Toad: *(eating)* A wonderful adventure. Such fun!

Ratty: Now, Toady, don't you see what an awful ass you've made of yourself? By your own admission you have been hand-cuffed, imprisoned, starved, chased, terrified out of your life, insulted, jeered at, and ignominiously flung into the water! Where's the amusement in that? Where does the fun come in? And all because you go and steal a motor-car. You know that you've never had anything but trouble from motor-cars from the moment you first set eyes on one.

Toad: *(appeasing)* I suppose you are quite right, Ratty! I've been a conceited old ass, I can quite see that; but now I'm going to be a good Toad and not do it any more. As for motor-cars, I've not been at all so keen about them since my last ducking in the river. *(Excited)* The fact is, while I was under the water, I had a sudden idea—a really brilliant idea—connected with motor-boats…

Rat: *(despairingly)* Oh no, not another …

Toad: There, there! don't take on so, old chap; it was only an idea and we won't talk any more about it now. We'll have our coffee, and then I'm going to stroll quietly down to Toad Hall and get into clothes of my own. I've had enough of adventures. I shall lead a quiet, steady, respectable life, pottering about my property, and improving it, and doing a little landscape gardening at times.

Rat: Stroll quietly down to Toad Hall? What are you talking about? Do you mean to say you haven't *heard*?

Toad: Heard what?

Rat: About the Stoats and Weasels. They've taken Toad Hall.

Toad: What! I don't believe… I mean…how? Why?

Rat: When you disappeared there a good deal talk, not only along the riverside, but in the Wild Wood, as well. Animals took sides, as always happens. The River-bankers stuck up for you and said you were just having an adventure and would be home soon enough. But the *Wild-Wooders* said hard things and they got very cocky and went about saying you were done for this time! You would never come back again, never, never!

Toad: *(angry)* That's the sort of nasty little beasts they are.

Rat: But we backed you, Mole and Badger and me, through thick and thin. We said you'd come back …and well, here you are.

Toad: But I don't understand, Ratty. If you told them that…

Rat: Well, they didn't listen, did they? They're weasels after all. Then one night—it was a *very* dark night, and blowing hard, too, and raining simply cats and dogs—a band of weasels, armed to the teeth, crept up the carriage-drive to the front entrance, while a troop of desperate ferrets, advanced through the kitchen-garden, and a company of skirmishing stoats occupied the conservatory and the billiard-room. Poor Mole and the Badger were sitting by the fire in the smoking-room, telling stories and suspecting nothing, when those bloodthirsty villains broke down the doors and rushed in upon them from every side. They made the best fight they could, but they were unarmed, and taken by surprise, and what can two animals do against hundreds? They beat them severely with sticks and turned them out into the cold and the wet, with many insulting and uncalled-for remarks! *(Pause)* And the *Wild-Wooders* have been living in Toad Hall ever since.

Toad: Oh, have they! Well I'll soon see about that!

Rat: It's no good, Toad! You'd had better sit down and finish your coffee.

But the Toad was off and there was no holding him. He marched rapidly down the road, a stick over his shoulder, fuming and muttering to himself in his anger. When he finally got near his front gate a long yellow ferret with a gun popped up from behind a bush and demanded: who goes there?

Toad: *(angry)* Stuff and nonsense! What do you mean by talking like that to me? Come out of that at once or I'll…

The ferret didn't say a word, but he brought his gun up to his shoulder and Bang! a bullet whistled over Toad's head.

The startled Toad scrambled to his feet and scampered off down the road as hard as he could; and as he ran he heard the ferret laughing and other nasty thin little laughs joining in.

Toad: *(breathless from running, then shouting)* Horrid things. Villains!   You won't stop me that easy!

So Toad got out Ratty's boat, and set off rowing up the river to where the garden front of Toad Hall came down to the water-side. Arriving within sight of his old home, he surveyed the land cautiously. He decided to try the Boat House first and warily paddled up to the mouth of the creek, and was just passing under the bridge, when ...

CRASH!

A great stone, dropped from above, smashed through the bottom of the boat. It filled and sank, and Toad found himself struggling in deep water. Looking up, he saw two stoats leaning over the parapet of the bridge and watching him with great glee and shouting it would be his head next time.

Rat: What did I tell you, Toad? They've got sentries posted, and they are all armed. But, no, you had to go and make a fool of yourself and what's worse, you've lost me my boat and I was very fond of that boat… Really, you are the most trying animal…it's a wonder you manage to keep any friends at all!

Toad: I'm sorry Ratty. You are right, you are always right. I have been a headstrong and a wilful Toad! Henceforth, believe me, I will be humble and submissive, and will take no action without your sage advice and full approval!

Rat: If that is really so, then my advice to you is to sit down and have your supper… and be very patient. We can do nothing until Mole and Badger come back and we've heard the latest news.

Toad: Oh how selfish of me not to ask before this…where are dear Mole and Badger?

Rat: Well may you ask! While you were galavanting about the country having adventures, those two poor devoted animals have been camping out in the open, in every sort of weather; watching over your house, patrolling your boundaries, keeping a constant eye on the stoats and the weasels, scheming and planning and contriving how to get your property back for you. You don't deserve to have such true and loyal friends, Toad. Some day, when it's too late, you'll be sorry you didn't value them more while you had them.

Toad: I'm an ungrateful beast, I know. Lets go and find them straight away…well perhaps, we'll have supper first…and then we won't waste a minute…

(<u>SFX</u>: Door opening)

Badger: Hello, Ratty. Aah Toad, I see you're back…

Toad: Badger! I've missed you, old chap. I must tell you all about…

Mole: Hello, Mr Toad.

Toad: Mole. Sweet, gentle Mole. How wonderful to see you both. *(Pause)* Though you look like…

Badger: Like we've been sleeping rough?

Mole: It was quite awful, but there was nothing else to be done in the circumstances.

Toad: Grand fellows. Who could ask for more loyal friends?

Mole: *(depressed)* I should say welcome home, I suppose. But what's the point if there's no home to welcome you in…

Rat: You look rather low, Badger. You always do on an empty stomach. Have some supper and then we can talk. You too, Mole.

Mole: Yes, please! It's marvellous to have you back again, Mr Toad. I mean we all heard the stories but never dreamed you'd escape. You must have been very clever…

Rat: Oh for heaven's sake, don't encourage him, Mole.

Toad: Clever? Oh, no! I'm not really clever, according to Ratty! I've only broken out of the strongest prison in the country, that's all! And captured a railway train and escaped on it, that's all! And disguised myself and gone about the country humbugging everybody, that's all! Oh no! I'm a stupid ass, I am according to

Ratty! Here, I'll tell you one or two of my little adventures, Mole, and you can judge for yourself!

Mole: Wonderful…but can you do it while I eat. Not a bite since breakfast! Oh my! Cold beef and pickles. Oh my, oh my…

Toad: First I disguised myself and simply walked past on the prison guards and then there was the Engine Driver…now he was easy to fool….

Mole: *(eating, mouth full)* Go on, Mr Toad…oh my, these pickles are delicious aren't they, Mr Badger.

(Badger grunts)

Rat: Toad, do be quiet, please! And I told you, don't egg him on, Mole. You know what's he's like…once he starts we'll never get to the important stuff. Now tell us, what's the position at Toad Hall?

Mole: The position's about as bad as it can be. Badger and I have been round and round the place, by night and by day; but it's always the same thing. Sentries posted everywhere, guns poked out at us, stones thrown at us; always an animal on the look-out, and when they see us, how they laugh! That's what annoyed us most, wasn't it, Mr Badger!

(Badger grunts)

Rat: It's a very difficult situation, but I think I see what Toad really ought to do. He ought to…

Mole: *(talking over him)* No, what he should to do is…

Toad: *(talking over both of them)* Well, I won't do either thing! I'm not going to be ordered about by you fellows! It's my house we're talking about, and I know exactly what to do, and I'll tell you. I'm going to…

Badger: *(loudly)* Be quiet all of you! *(Pause)* That's better. I'm feeling like myself again. Lovely bit of pie that, Rat…Now, what was I going to say…oh yes. Toad, you are a bad and troublesome little animal!

Toad: I think that's a little harsh, Badger. I mean, I have many good qualities…

Badger: They are well hidden! What do you think your father would have said if he had been here and known of all your goings on?

(Toad cries loudly)

Badger: There, there! Stop crying, Toad. What Mole said is quite true. The stoats are on guard, at every point, and they make the best sentinels in the world. It's quite useless to think of attacking the place. They're too strong for us.

Toad: *(still crying)* Then it's all over. I'll never see my dear Toad Hall again!

Badger: There are more ways of getting back a place than taking it by storm. I haven't said my last word yet. *(Pause)* I am going to tell you all a great secret. *(Pause)* There—is—an—underground—passage, that leads from the river-bank, quite near here, right up into the middle of Toad Hall.

Toad: Oh, nonsense! Badger. You've been listening to those yarns they spin in the public-houses round here. I know every inch of Toad Hall, inside and out. There's nothing of the sort, I assure you!

Badger: I tell you there is. Your father discovered it before you were born.

Toad: He never told me.

Badger: "Don't let my son know about it,' he said. 'He's a good boy, but simply can't hold his tongue. "

Toad: Well, perhaps I am a bit of a talker. But I am a popular fellow with the gift of conversation. My friends all expect witty stories. ..

Rat: Be quiet, Toad. It's a pity you don't have the gift of silence. How is this passage going to help us Badger?

Badger: Now that is a good question, Rat! I got Otter to disguise himself as a sweep and call at the back-door of Toad Hall, asking for a job…

Otter: Is there a job here?

Sergeant Stoat: On your way!

Otter: That's not very friendly! *(Big sniff)* What's that delightful smell?

Sergeant Stoat: On your way, I said.

Otter: Is that tongue baking? And Lobster? There must be something special planned?

Sergeant Stoat: There's a banquet for the Chief Weasel's birthday. And we don't want the likes of you hanging about! Now get going or I'll hit you with my stick.

Otter: Alright, alright…there's no need to be unpleasant. I'll go, but before I do, any chance of a little snack for the road?

Mole: A banquet?

Badger: Yes, and the Chief Weasel insisting all his followers gather in the dining-hall to celebrate it. They'll be eating and drinking and laughing and carrying on, suspecting nothing. No guns, no swords, no sticks, no arms of any sort whatever!

Mole: Will the sentinels still be posted.

Badger: Only the stoats, my young friend, because the weasels don't like to socialise with them…but they won't bother us. That very useful tunnel goes under them and leads right up to the butler's pantry, next to the dining-hall!

Toad: You mean…

Mole: *(excited)* We will creep out quietly into the butler's pantry…

Rat: *(excited)* …with our pistols and swords and sticks….

Badger: .. and rush in on them.

Toad: …and whack 'em, and whack 'em, and whack 'em!

Rat: Steady, Toad. You almost fell out of that chair

Badger: Very well, then, our plan is settled. Now it's off to bed for a good night's rest and we'll make all arrangements in the morning.

Toad, of course, went off to bed dutifully thinking he was much too excited to sleep, but the moment his head hit the pillow he was snoring happily and dreaming of standing triumphantly in the Dining Room of Toad Hall, all his friends gathered round him saying what a clever Toad he was…

He slept till a late hour next morning, and by the time he got down he found that the other animals had finished their breakfast. Mole had slipped off somewhere by himself, without telling any one where he was going. Badger sat in the arm-chair, reading the paper, and not concerning himself in the slightest about what was going to happen that very evening. Ratty, on the other hand, was running round the room busily, with his arms full of weapons of every kind, distributing them in four little heaps on the floor.

Rat; Here's-a-sword-for-the-Rat, here's-a-sword-for-the-Mole, here's-a-sword-for-the-Toad, here's-a-sword-for-the-Badger! Here's-a-pistol-for-the-Rat, here's-a-pistol-for-the-Mole, here's-a-pistol-for-the-Toad, here's-a-pistol-for-the-Badger!"

Badger: I can assure you we shan't want any swords or pistols, Rat. Weasels are very cowardly things. We four, with our sticks, will clear the floor of the lot of them in five minutes. I dare say, I'd could have done it by myself, only I didn't want to deprive you fellows of the fun!

Rat: It always pays to be on the safe side!

Toad: Is there any breakfast, Ratty.

Rat: There's some toast on the table!

Toad: But there's no jam.

Rat: *(frustrated)* Is jam all you can think about on a day like this.

Toad: We'll, no…there's eggs, and sausages and…

Rat: Aaargh

At that moment, Mole came tumbling into the room, looking very pleased.

Mole: I've been having such fun! I've been getting a rise out of the stoats!

Rat: *(annoyed)* I hope you were careful, Moley? We can't afford any slips up

Mole: I should hope so, too. I got the idea when I went into the kitchen and found that old washerwoman-dress that Mr Toad came home in yesterday. I put it on, and the bonnet as well, and the shawl, and off I went to Toad Hall, as bold as you please. The sentries were on the look-out, of course, with their guns. ..

Stoat: Who goes there?

Mole: 'Good morning, gentlemen!' I say, very respectful. 'Want any washing done to-day?'

Stoat: Go away, washerwoman! We don't do any washing on duty.

Mole: Or any other time, by the look of you, I tell them *(Laughs)* Well some of the stoats turned quite pink at that , and the Sergeant in charge stared at me and spoke very short.

Sergeant Stoat: Run away, washerwoman, run away! Don't keep my men idling and talking on their posts.

Mole: Run away?' says I; 'it won't be me that'll be running away, in a very short time from now!

Stoat: What? What was that you were saying?

Mole: I could see them pricking up their ears and looking at each other.

Sergeant Stoat: Never mind *her*; she doesn't know what she's talking about.

Mole: "'Oh! don't I?' I says . 'Well, let me tell you this. I hear a thing or two while I'm doing the washing and I happen to know a hundred bloodthirsty badgers, armed with rifles, are going to attack Toad Hall this very night. Six boatloads of rats, with pistols and cutlasses, will come up the river as well; while a mighty body of toads, known as the Die-hards, or the Death-or-Glory Toads, will storm the orchard and carry everything before them, yelling for vengeance. There won't be much left of you to wash, by the time they're done, unless you clear out now, while you have the chance!' Then I ran away laughing and when I was out of sight, I hid in a hedge. From there I could see they were all nervous.

Stoat: Boat loads of rats!.

Sergeant Stoat: Steady, son.

Stoat: Death or glory toads…

Sergeant Stoat: Remember your training, lad!

Stoat: But that's just like the weasels, Sarge; they'll be comfortable in the Banqueting Hall, feasting and singing songs while we're out here in the cold, being cut to pieces by bloodthirsty Badgers!

Toad: Oh, you silly ass, Mole! You've ruined everything!

Badger: Nonsense! Mole, I think you have more sense in your little finger than some other animals have in the whole of their bodies. You have created an excellent diversion for us. I am beginning to have great hopes for you.

The Toad was simply wild with jealousy about all the praise being offered and none of it to him, particularly as he couldn't make out for the life of him what the Mole had done that was so clever; but before he could show temper and expose himself to the Badger's sarcasm, the bell rang for lunch and he had to hurriedly finish his toast so he'd be ready for the next meal.

Transition

When it began to grow dark, Ratty, summoned them back into the parlour, stood each of them up alongside of his little heap, and proceeded to dress them up for the coming expedition. First, there was a belt to go round each animal, and then a sword to be stuck into each belt, and then a cutlass on the other side to balance it. Then a pair of pistols, a policeman's truncheon, several sets of handcuffs, some bandages and sticking-plaster, and a flask and a sandwich-case.

Badger: All right, Ratty, that's enough.

Rat: I don't want to forget anything, Badger

Badger: I told you I'll being doing all I need to tonight with this stick. *(Pause)* Alright chaps, it's time to go. And Toad, none of your usual chatter …

Badger led them along the river for a little way and then suddenly swung himself over the edge into a hole in the bank, a little above the water. Mole and the Rat followed silently, swinging themselves successfully into the hole; but when it came to Toad's turn, of course he managed to slip and fall into the water with a loud splash and a squeal of alarm. He was hauled out by his friends, rubbed down and wrung out hastily.

Toad: *(spluttering)* I *am* really quite sick and tired of the water! I may not ever have a bath again.

Badger: *(angry)* Toad, I suspect you'll be the ruin of this mission! The next time you make a fool of yourself we'll leave you behind! Come on, we haven't all night.

Toad: *(stage whisper)* Badger is really a tyrant, Ratty. I mean it's cold and dark in here. And I'm still very wet.

Rat: *(snaps)* For once in your life, be quiet Toad!

Toad: *(stage whisper)* Ratty, is quite the tyrant as well, isn't he. Mole.

(SFX: Muffled sound of a party - singing, shouting)

Badger: *(whispered)* We're here.

Mole: They seem to be having a splendid time.

Rat: We'll soon put a stop to that!

Toad: Oh dear…

Mole: What the matter, Toad?

Toad: It sounds like there is quite a lot of them …

Badger: All the more to thrash with my stick! To battle, men.

They hurried along the passage till it came to a full stop and they found themselves standing under the trap-door that led up into the butler's pantry. Such a tremendous noise was going on in the Banqueting Hall now that there was little danger of their being overheard.

Badger: Alright…all together, now. PUSH!

(Grunting sound as they all lift the trap door)

Hoisting each other up, they found themselves standing in the pantry, with only a door between them and the Banqueting Hall. The noise that emerged was simply deafening. Cheering and hammering and speeches about Toad and how he was such a kind host to allow them to stay in his home, that were followed by shrieks of laughter.

Toad: *(angry)* Let me at them…I'll…I'll triturate them. I'll pulverise them.

Badger: Hold your temper for a minute! Get ready, all of you! *(Longish pause)* Now…The hour has come!

And with that, he flung the door open and the four friends charged in.

(<u>SFX</u>: Four shouting charge, surprise squeals from the weasels)

What squealing and squeaking and screeching filled the air!

Terrified weasels hid behind furniture and jumped out of the windows! Ferrets rushed wildly for the fireplace and got hopelessly jammed in the chimney! Tables and chairs were overturned and glass and china shattered on the floor.

And in the middle of it all, stood the four heroes of the adventure. The mighty Badger, his whiskers bristling, his great cudgel whistling through the air; Mole, black and grim, brandishing his stick and shouting his awful war-cry

Mole: *(shouting)* BEWARE THE MOLE.

Ratty, desperate and determined, his belt bulging with weapons of every age and every variety; Toad, frenzied with excitement and injured pride, swollen to twice his ordinary size, leaping into the air and emitting Toad-whoops that chilled them to the marrow!

Toad: Your kind host, am I? Well, take that! And that! What no laughing now?

They were just four in all, but as Badger had predicted, to the the panic-stricken and cowardly weasels the Hall seemed full of monstrous animals: grey, black, brown and yellow, whooping and flourishing enormous cudgels.

They broke and fled with squeals of terror and dismay, this way and that, anywhere to get out of reach of those terrible sticks…and just like that, the battle was over.

Badger: Mole, look outside and see what those stoat-sentries are doing. I've an idea that, after the story you told them, they won't be giving us much trouble to-night!

Mole: *(still excited)* If they do, they feel the wrath of the washerwoman! *(Shouting)* BEWARE THE MOLE!

Rat: Brave fellow.

Badger: Good comrade in arms.

Mole: (muted, in distance) Beware the Mole!

Badger: Look lively, Toad ! We've got your house back for you, and you don't offer us so much as a sandwich.

Toad felt rather hurt that the Badger and Ratty didn't say pleasant things about him: what a fine fellow he was, and how splendidly he had fought. He was, in fact, rather pleased with himself.

Toad: *(trying to beg praise)* Did you see what I did with the Chief Weasel, Badger? Chased him out of the window with my big stick. *(Laugh)* I expect he's still running. He won't laugh at Toad again.

Badger: Yes, yes…very good. But what about that sandwich? Battle makes a chap hungry.

Toad: *(disappointed at the lack of praise)* I expect, I could find some jelly and trifle.

Badger: There's some lobster salad that hasn't fallen on the floor.

Rat: And that slice of tongue over there. It's hardly been touched! Hop to, Toad.

Toad: *(annoyed)* I'm not a serving girl!

Rat: Just a washerwoman, then. *(Laughs)*

Mole: *(distant)* It's all over. *(Then closer)* From what I can make out, as soon as the stoats heard the shrieks inside the hall, they threw down their rifles and ran. But even though they had a head start, those cowardly weasels passed them. *(Laughs)* They've all disappeared into the Wild Wood now and I've got their rifles. So they won't be coming back anytime soon.

Badger: What an excellent and brave animal you are, Mole!

Toad: I bet the Chief Weasel was running faster than all of them. Wasn't he, Mole? And looking over his shoulder to see if the Terrible Toad was in pursuit.

Badger: *(dismissive)* Hrumph...we'll sit down for supper and have no more of the battle talk.

And with that pronouncement, the four animals sat round the table and ate a very hearty meal, before heading to bed for a well deserved rest.

Transition

The following morning, Toad, who had overslept as usual, came down to breakfast disgracefully late and found on the table a certain quantity of egg-shells, some fragments of cold and leathery toast, a coffee-pot half empty and really, very little else. Through the French windows of the breakfast-room he could see Mole and Ratty sitting in wicker chairs on the lawn, evidently telling each other stories; roaring with laughter and kicking their short legs up in the air. Badger, who was in an arm-chair and deep in the morning paper, looked up and nodded

Badger: I'm sorry, Toad. I'm afraid there's a heavy morning's work in front of you. You see, we really ought to have a banquet at once, to celebrate this affair. It's expected of you—in fact, it's the rule.

Toad: It is?

Badger: *(firmly)* It is!

Toad: *(sarcastically)* All right! Anything to oblige. Though why on earth you should want to have a banquet in the morning I do not understand.

Badger: *(snapping)* Don't pretend to be stupider than you really are and don't chuckle and splutter in your coffee while you're talking. It's not manners. You know I mean the banquet will be at night. But the invitations will have to be sent off at once. Now sit down at that table and write to all our friends.

Toad: What! Me stop indoors and write a lot of rotten letters on a jolly morning like this, when I want to go around my property and set everything and everybody to rights. Certainly not! I'll be… *(Pause)* Why, of course, dear Badger! What is my pleasure compared with that of others! You wish it done, and it shall be done. I will happily sacrifice this fair morning on the altar of duty and friendship!

Badger looked at him suspiciously, but Toad's frank, open countenance made it difficult to see any unworthy motive in this change of attitude. He nodded and headed the direction of the kitchen, and as soon as the door had closed behind him, Toad hurried to the writing-table. A fine idea had occurred to him while he was talking. He would write the invitations and he would take care to mention the leading part he had taken in the fight and how he had laid the Chief Weasel flat… and he would hint at his adventures and what triumphs he'd had. Then on the fly-leaf he would set out a sort of a programme of entertainment for the evening.

Toad: First there will be a speech by Toad. Then there will be an address by Toad on our prison system and water ways. After another short speech by Toad, there will be a poem, written and read …by Toad! Yes, a splendid evening.

When the other animals came back for lunch, very boisterous and breezy after a morning on the river, they expected to find a sulky and depressed Toad, but instead found him very uppish and inflated, which instantly made them suspect something was up.

Toad: Well, look after yourselves, fellows! Ask for anything you want! I'm off to walk the gardens. I have some thinking to do.

Rat: Thinking about what?

Toad: Speeches, and such. They don't write themselves, you know.

Rat: Hold up there, Toad. Mole, grab his other arm.

Toad: What are you doing? Unhand me!

Mole: Don't struggle, Mr Toad. You'll hurt yourself.

Toad: Outrage!

Rat: Sit him down on that chair. Now don't you move, Toady! *(Pause)* Will you tell him Badger?

Badger: Now, look here, Toad, about this banquet, we want you to understand clearly, once and for all, that there are going to be no speeches, no poems and no songs. Try and grasp the fact that on this occasion we're not arguing with you; we're telling you.

Toad: Just one *little* song?

Badger: No, not *one*.

Toad: A poem then …and maybe a short speech to welcome everyone…

Badger: NO. NO. NO… you know very well that your poems and songs are all conceit and boasting and vanity; and your speeches… well they're nothing but self-praise and—and…and gross exaggeration and…and..

Rat: GAS! *(Sympathetically)* It's for your own good, Toady. You know you *must* turn over a new leaf sooner or later, and now seems as good a time as ever.

Toad: *(almost in tears)* Of course, Ratty. You're right. You are both right.

Badger: Good chap.

Toad: *(quietly)* I think I'll still go for a walk in the gardens, if you don't mind. It's such a lovely day.

And, pressing his handkerchief to his face, he left the room, a dejected figure.

Mole: He looks so sad.

Badger: He'll get over it soon enough. Toad is a resilient animal. He can bounce back from anything.

Rat: Still, I feel like a bit of a brute, Badger.

Badger: I know. I know. But the thing had to be done. You saw that invitation on his desk. Speeches, and addresses and poems. All by Toad. He has to live here and be respected. What do you think would happen after all that?

Rat: He'd be a laughing-stock.

Mole: But surely one song wouldn't matter? And it would make him so happy.

Rat: Toad would never stop at one. It's not in his nature.

Badger: Like friendship. He just expects it but does nothing to earn it.

Mole: But we are his friends and I, for one, would not laugh at his speech!

Badger: You are a good natured animal, Mole. Perhaps the best of all of us. But you're young. It's for his own good, You'll have to trust us on this matter. And Ratty, I think we better keep an eye on Toady. If history tells us anything, his promises to change are short lived.

Transition

The hour for the Banquet drew near, and Toad, poor, sad Toad, dipped his hairbrush in the water-jug, parted his hair in the middle, and plastered it down very straight and sleek on each side of his face. Then unlocking the door, he went quietly down the stairs to greet his guests.

(<u>SFX</u>: Cheering)

Toad: Oh my. Why, thank you.

Otter: Hello, you old Toad.

Toad: Otter? So nice of you to come.

Otter: Wouldn't have missed it. Fantastic grub. And plenty of it. Couldn't be happier . I've been hearing about your courage and your cleverness and your fighting qualities. Can't wait to hear the speech.

Toad: I'm sorry Otter. I won't be talking about that. I won't be talking about myself tonight.

Otter: What! *(Laughs)* That's a fine joke. Toad not talking. *(Laughing …them suddenly distracted.)* Is that Yorkshire Pudding over there? It is… and just in time. I'm starving!

And so it was all night. Animals asking him when he was going to make his speech and then walking away laughing, when they were told he wasn't. Eventually, exhausted by the effort required to remain humble, Toad curled up in the big chair by the fireplace, far away from the celebrations. …and that's where his three friends found him, staring pathetically into the dying fire, wishing that the Banquet was over and he could go to bed.

Mole: Why are you hiding here, Mr Toad? You should be enjoying your party.

Toad: *(depressed)* Don't want to!

Rat: Oh buck up, Toady. After all, you've got your home back and you've had a stack adventures. Is that what it is? That you can't tell everyone about them.

Toad: No…well, maybe at first. After our conservation, I admit I was very annoyed and scheming all afternoon. I wrote speeches and song…even a poem I'm rather proud of. But it's not that…

Badger: So what is it, then?

Toad: It's…it's…that all night people have been asking me to speak about myself and they don't believe it when I say I won't. They just assume that I will take the credit. I've realised.. *(Pause)*… I'm conceited and foolish and…a braggart.

Mole: Of course, you are…

Toad: *(shocked at the agreement)* What?

Mole: You are all those thing, Toad, but you are also kind and generous and great fun.

Rat: All good qualities in a friend.

Toad: Is that true, Badger?

Badger: Very true. You can be a frustrating animal at times and there's no doubt you have your faults, but we all have those. All in all, you have a good heart, Toad. We wouldn't have helped, if you didn't.

Toad: *(emotional)* Oh Badger. Oh Ratty. Oh Mole. I'm sorry, I've been such a bad friend. I promise to be better from now on…I will change, just you wait and see. Humility will be my new watch word!

Rat: Let's not get carried away. After all, you are still Toad.

Mole: I think you should make a speech.

Toad: Really? No I don't think so. The new Toad doesn't need to make speeches.

Mole: Everyone is expecting it and they'll be terribly disappointed if you don't.

Toad: I don't want disappoint my guests…well, maybe it would be alright if I keep it short…what do you think, Badger?

Badger: Go on then! *(Laughs)* We were on a fool's errand if we thought we'd keep you quiet all night…

And with that, a newly energised Toad jumped to his feet and with a series of coughs and whistles, summoned the attention of the crowd.

Toad: *(projecting)* Just a few words, friends…

Rat: Well here we go, we'd better settle in…

Mole: *(good humoured)* … for the night, I think!

Toad: Dear friends, wonderful friends, many of you have been asking me to speak about my adventures and about the great Battle of Toad Hall. You want to be regaled with stories of courage and cleverness.

Otter: *(mouth full)* Hear, hear…by the way, is there anymore of this lobster tail?

Toad: But…but *(Pause)* The truth is that Badger there, was the master mind and Mole and Ratty bore the brunt of the fighting. I merely served in the ranks and did little or nothing!

Rat: *(surprised)* Well I never thought I'd see the day..

Badger: He really is a different Toad!

Mole: *(clapping hands lightly in delight)* A wonderful Toad. A humble Toad.

Toad: I have no more to say, except enjoy yourselves. There is plenty of jelly and trifle left.

Otter: Wonderful…wonderful!

Toad bowed to his shocked guests and began to walk as humbly as he could out of the room. But, then, he stopped at the door and raised a hand in front of him as if to make a point.

Toad: I suppose there's one thing I could do before bidding you all goodnight. You see there's a poem I wrote and I did spend an awful lot of time on it... Perhaps you'd like to hear just a little *(Laughs)* Vroom, vroom. Vroom, vroom.

Yes, it was true that Toad had changed, but as Ratty had said, he was still Toad!

www.ingramcontent.com/pod-product-compliance
Lightning Source LLC
Chambersburg PA
CBHW070309010526
44107CB00056B/2535